Self-Help Kit

What to do following a death

Guidance Manual

by Cruse Bereavement Care

Using this Lawpack Kit

This Lawpack Kit contains information and advice to help you cope with both the administrative procedures and the emotions of bereavement following the death of a loved one.

The information in this Kit has been carefully compiled from reliable sources but its accuracy is not guaranteed, as regulations and laws may change or be subject to differing interpretations.

Neither this nor any other publication can take the place of a solicitor when it comes to important legal matters following a death. This Lawpack Kit is sold with the understanding that the publisher, author and retailer are not engaged in rendering legal services. If legal advice or other expert assistance is required, the services of a competent professional should be sought.

Common sense should determine whether you need the assistance of a solicitor rather than relying solely on the information and forms in this Lawpack Kit.

Contents

Using this Lawpack Kit   2

Helping yourself and others after a death   5
Understanding bereavement   5
The varying experiences of bereavement   6
Your health   6
Family and friends   7
Grieving children   8
Coping at work   9
When to seek help   9
The future   10

When someone dies: the official procedures   11
Deaths in a hospital or hospice   11
Deaths at home or elsewhere   11
Sudden death   12
Registering a death   12
Deaths abroad   16
Deaths in the armed forces   17
Organ donation   18

Post-mortems and inquests   19
Post-mortems   19
Inquests   22

Funerals   25
First choices   25
Finding a funeral director   26
What you should expect from a funeral director   26
Green funerals, woodland burials and home burials   27
Burial at sea   27
Designing a funeral ceremony   27
Arranging a cremation   28
Arranging a burial   29
Funeral costs   30
After the funeral   31
Memorials   32

Finance and property   33
State benefits   33
Bank accounts   35
Housing   35

Dealing with the estate 36

Personal and company pensions 42

Financial planning in changed circumstances after the death 43

Looking to the future 44

Your landmarks 44

Ways of commemorating the person who has died 44

If memories are difficult 45

The future 45

Useful contacts 46

Resources for children and young people 51

Template letters 53

Template letter to building society 53

Template letter to pension scheme 54

Loose leaf documents:

Checklist – what to do following a death

Looking after yourself and other people

Funerals – some ideas and issues

In the unlikely event of any missing loose-leaf forms in your copy of this Kit, please call Lawpack on **020 7394 4040**.

Please note we are not authorised to give legal, accounting or tax advice.

This Lawpack Kit is 'web enabled', meaning that additional government leaflets and forms can be downloaded from Lawpack's website. To access this extra information, all you have to do is register on the Lawpack website at www. lawpack.co.uk and then click on the web enablement link on our home page. You then enter the activation code printed below when requested.

Registration code: **P2250704491**

Please note that this Kit is fully functional without the user having to register or use this service.

Helping yourself and others after a death

As a reader of this Kit, it is likely that you have been affected by the death of someone close to you. If the person was a loved one, the material in this Kit aims to help you to get through this difficult time. If you are reading this because a friend has been bereaved, it will help you to help them. This section of the Kit highlights the emotional impact of bereavement.

Understanding bereavement

We all know that we must die and losing someone we love has always been a painful experience, and it will never be otherwise. The experiences of loss and grief are universal, yet everyone reacts to them in their own way.

Coping

Losing a loved one is bad enough but, inevitably, the death also brings other changes. Unwelcome formalities have to be coped with, and changed circumstances accepted. Life will be different.

Emotions

This section of the Kit is for you to read if you would like some help in accepting or dealing with your overpowering feelings, especially if the death is recent. Every death has its own unique circumstances. If the person you loved had an illness from which you knew that he or she was not going to recover, you may have had some opportunity to prepare for your loss. If the death was sudden, you may be feeling that you had no chance at all to say goodbye. Whatever your situation, you may wish to see the body, whether in the hospital mortuary or at the funeral director's premises. There are many different expectations and traditions for dealing with this, and you should ask hospital staff or the funeral director to help you achieve what is right for you and others who were close to the person who has died.

There is no prescription to deal with grief. The first thing to say is that if you are feeling shocked, sad, overwhelmed or at a loss, this is entirely normal. You are not going mad or becoming ill. It is important, though, to look after yourself as well as you can at this time, because grief may have an impact on your physical health as well as on your emotions.

The information about bereavement given here reflects what is generally known about it, but please do not expect your feelings to conform to any pattern; everyone is different. The first few days are often confusing and difficult to get through. When someone dies, a relationship is lost forever and we have to find a way to cope with the future, however hard that may feel. We are complicated creatures, and any difficulties in our relationship with the person who has died are likely to make bereavement harder to deal with.

The varying experiences of bereavement

One purpose of this Kit is to give you easy access to what is known about bereavement, so please use it to cope in your own way. You may be reading this because of the death of a loved one after a long illness; perhaps you knew that recovery was impossible. Despite this, the death may still have come as a shock. The feelings of shock and numbness are very common after deaths from all causes; sometimes numbness helps us to cope by providing a little protection from overwhelming feelings. Bereavement may make us feel unsafe, sad, regretful, angry, guilty, empty, or without purpose or hope.

'My reaction was complete incomprehension. One minute I'm angry and the next minute I can't stop crying. I feel nothing. I feel so depressed, like life has no meaning and I can't go on. I hear and see her. What is wrong with me?'

'I didn't really want to think about it too much. I really didn't want to think that it was Peter's body. I didn't want the full horror to register.'

We have highlighted these reactions, not to predict your experiences, but to provide reassurance that in bereavement, difficult feelings are normal.

You will sometimes hear people refer to 'stages of grief' – this can be helpful in emphasising that things will change and that you will not always feel the way you do now. Be aware, though, that what you will experience is likely to be more like ebb and flow – two steps forward and one step back. How you react will also be affected by your roles in life – whether you are an adult who has lost a parent, whether your partner has died, and by many other aspects of your own situation.

'I was desperate. I'd never felt like this before.'

You are not losing control, or going mad; these are normal (even if overwhelming) reactions and they will become less intense over time.

Your health

It is very important at this time to look after your physical health in the best way you can. Physical symptoms may be part of your bereavement reaction, and it may be hard to get enough sleep or to eat properly, especially if you have others to look after. It is important, at this time, to try to eat as regularly as you can, to rest when you need to and, generally, not to ask too much of yourself.

You may find yourself dreaming about the person who has died or (especially if you witnessed a violent death) you may experience flashbacks. If your bereavement seems to be particularly difficult, you may need to ask for further help – see page 9 for more information.

Many bereaved people visit their GP immediately after the death or later in bereavement, and they find this helpful. Your GP will be able to discuss with you whether medication may help – in dealing with sleeplessness, for example – although it is important to remember that bereavement is a natural process and not a treatable illness. Because you are bereaved, you are likely to feel sad and unhappy. This is not the same as clinical depression, but if you feel that you are becoming seriously depressed, then you should seek medical advice. If you become worried about your use of alcohol to 'cope', and this dependency does not go away, then talking to a friend or to your doctor about what help is available may be a good first step.

Family and friends

Your family and friends will be more important to you than ever at this difficult time and, of course, you may have lost the person who matters most in the world to you. People who can accept your feelings, be there when you need them and understand when you need to be alone, will be your greatest support. Some people find it a great support to have someone who can help with the many practical tasks which arise after a death.

In bereavement there are many pressures and when several family members are grieving, they will not all grieve in the same way. Most people can understand and accept this, but do not be surprised if sometimes family members find this difficult. It is worth doing what you can to make sure that close family members have a chance to discuss essential decisions (e.g. what kind of funeral should be held), although, of course, the known wishes of the person who has died, or of the family member closest to them, may need to be acted upon. Sadly, it is not always possible to reach agreement and strong feelings may be aroused. If this is the case, it is worth thinking about whether there is a trusted person who may be able to help others avoid lasting bitterness.

The friend who is able to stay with you through the rollercoaster of grief is your greatest ally; to have your feelings and wishes respected is what will be of most help to you.

If you are reading this because you want to help a bereaved person, do not be put off by his or her sadness or overwhelming feelings. The simple ways in which people show concern for one another will still work – you do not have to be an expert.

How to help a bereaved person

- Just listen – you probably have not got the answers.
- Do not say, 'I know how you feel'.
- He or she has chosen you, so do not run away.
- Crying is part of recovery. Do not say, 'Would you like a tissue?'

- There is no timescale for grief, so never say, 'You should be over it by now'.

- Do not cheer up a bereaved person in order to spare yourself discomfort.

- Do not deny the other person's feelings.

- Ask/talk about the person who has died.

- Be aware of special dates, such as anniversaries.

- Do not recite or compare your own experiences.

- Do not make assumptions about what your friend is or is not feeling.

- If you are really worried, encourage your friend to seek help.

Grieving children

There are many resources for grieving children – you can find some on page 51. Again, some very basic principles will help:

- Like adults, children appreciate having their thoughts and feelings acknowledged.

- Trying to shield children from the facts and from distress will not work and can lead to situations where their imaginings are worse than reality.

- Explanations should be given in words which are appropriate for the child's age.

- Children are as vulnerable as adults to the ebb and flow of feelings in bereavement.

Sometimes children may find that drawing or playing out events or feelings helps them to come to terms with their loss. It is worthwhile to encourage your child in whatever mode of expression he or she finds best. Bear in mind that younger children may have really practical misunderstandings – they may wonder, for example, if cremation hurts. Guilt may also be a problem if the child or young person has regrets about the way he or she has treated the person who has died, or mistakenly worries that it may have been his or her fault.

If you have lost a partner and your child a parent, this will be a particularly difficult time. If there is a family member or friend who is trusted by you and your child, he or she may be able to provide invaluable support. It is best to discuss with your child his or her feelings and wishes about attending the funeral and, if you can, to involve your child in designing an aspect of the ceremony which is important to him or her (e.g. a child may like to place a letter in the coffin or, if he or she feels able, to read or say something at the ceremony). Memories are precious and later much comfort may be provided by memory boxes or photo albums, or by talking and writing about the person who has died.

As with adults, it is important to seek help if a child appears to be having particular difficulty in coping with bereavement. The child's school should be told what has happened, preferably by involving a teacher with whom there is a good relationship. Birthdays, anniversaries and occasions such as Mother's Day or Father's Day are times when a child may need special care.

Older children may find studying difficult and they may need to ask for extra time to complete projects. The resources list on page 51 includes sources of peer support for young people.

Coping at work

Employers vary widely in the amount of compassionate leave they are prepared or able to grant, and this may be paid or unpaid. It may be specified in your contract of employment. Inevitably, if you have lost someone close, you will need time off work. You may need time off to arrange and/or attend the funeral, to visit relatives, to sort out practical issues, to rest at a stressful time and to ensure that you are fit for work.

It is best to let your employer know what has happened as soon as you can, and to keep in touch. If you are not well enough to return at the time expected, it may be appropriate to visit your GP to ask for a certificate, as you may qualify for sickness pay (which should be specified in your contract).

If you work for a large organisation, you may be able to benefit from the support of Human Resources, the Staff Welfare department, or an Employee Assistance Programme. If these resources are available in your company, they should have bereavement care procedures for staff.

When you return to work, it may be helpful to enlist a trusted colleague to let others know about any preferences you have about how you would like the situation to be dealt with. If you are unable to return to work within a reasonable time, and this causes difficulty, you may wish to seek advice about your employment rights from a trade union, if you are a member, or from one of the sources of information listed in our 'Useful contacts' section on page 46.

If you work for a small business, or run your own, especially if it is a family concern, you will have particular difficulties to deal with, especially if an essential member of the business has died. Reviewing your options with a friend or business colleague may help.

When to seek help

 ### Support during bereavement

During bereavement we would all like to be heard and understood, and many people find that family and friends are able to provide this support. Sometimes, however, they too are grieving and we then need external support to provide reassurance that our reactions are 'normal'. Listed in the 'Useful contacts' section of this Kit (on page 46) are bereavement organisations whose trained volunteers and staff are able to listen objectively and compassionately, reducing worries about burdening family and friends.

 ### When the effects of bereavement may be more serious

You may want to seek some outside help if you are feeling or doing some of the things below:

- If you feel that you cannot handle intense feelings or if you are worried by your physical symptoms.

- If you feel that your emotions are not falling into place over a period of time and you feel chronic tension, confusion, emptiness or exhaustion.

- If, for a long period, you have to keep active in order to avoid painful feelings.

- If you continue to have nightmares and poor sleep.

- If you do not have a person or group with whom you can share your emotions, but you feel that you need to.

- If your relationships seem to be suffering badly or sexual problems develop.

- If you have accidents.

- If you continue to smoke, drink or take drugs in excess after the bereavement.

- If your work performance suffers.

- If those around you are particularly vulnerable.

- If you, as a helper, are suffering from exhaustion.

These are examples of what can happen as a result of more complicated grief reactions, which are more likely where:

- the person died in a way which was untimely, or violent, or was the result of an event involving multiple deaths;

- the relationship with the person who died was difficult;

- the bereaved person had other traumatic life experiences or is experiencing other personal or psychological difficulties.

Most people have heard of post-traumatic stress disorder, which involves intense recollections of the traumatic event and recurring unpleasant symptoms, such as flashbacks, inability to concentrate, irritability, and so on. It is essential, if you feel that you or a bereaved friend may be suffering in this way, to seek medical help, as expert treatment is available. Similarly, whilst there is a difference between feeling sad and being depressed, if there is any danger that you are suffering from clinical depression, medical advice and correct treatment are essential.

The future

Necessarily, this Kit has focused on difficult feelings and the problems loss may bring, but it is not the intention of this Kit to foster hopelessness. For most people, although life will never be the same again, the future does have positive things to offer, however difficult it may seem now. Memories of the person who has died are precious, and may prove a great comfort. Although bereavement is intensely stressful, it is possible for you to move forward to a positive, although different, future.

When someone dies: the official procedures

This section provides you with an overview of the procedures which have to be followed when someone dies. Some procedures are specific to England & Wales, Northern Ireland or Scotland. Many local authorities now have good websites giving information about local services and facilities and it is worth looking at any information available for your area. Go to your local authority home page and search on 'bereavement'.

When someone has died, the death certificate is an essential document which enables other essential procedures to happen. All deaths must be registered to enable the cause of death to be recorded as clearly as possible and to enable trends in population and public health to be monitored.

Deaths in a hospital or hospice

Many hospitals have a Senior Manager and/or Bereavement Co-ordinator who is responsible for explaining post-death procedures to bereaved people. They can provide you with useful literature and inform you about the arrangement for the storage and release of the body.

The person recorded as the next of kin or closest friend/relative will be informed of the death and arrangements will be made to return the possessions of the person who has died. The hospital will arrange for the body to be transported from where the death occurred in the hospital to the hospital's mortuary. The body will remain in the mortuary until it is taken away for the funeral.

In some cases, the medical team may request permission to carry out a post-mortem (also called an 'autopsy') to determine the cause of death, or for research purposes.

In a hospice, the staff will have worked with the dying person and his or her family to prepare for the death and they will make arrangements immediately afterwards, including providing the certificate of the cause of death.

Deaths at home or elsewhere

In many cases, the doctor, who normally attended the person who has died, will be able to certify the cause of death. He or she will issue two documents:

1. A medical certificate for submission to the Registrar of Deaths. There is no fee for this certificate (Form B).

2. A formal notice. This is the document that confirms that the doctor has issued a medical certificate of death and also gives you the information about how to register the death.

Sudden death

In cases of sudden death (e.g. in a road crash) or unexpected death (wherever it occurred) it may be necessary for the doctor to refer the death to the Coroner, who may order a post-mortem examination. A sudden or unexplained death may also give rise to an investigation by the police. Following the post-mortem, the Coroner may issue the death certificate or he or she may decide that an inquest is required. Please see page 22 for further details about inquests and Coroners.

Registering a death

Deaths must normally be registered within five days. Registration of the death can be delayed for a further nine days if the Registrar receives written confirmation that a medical certificate of the cause of death has been signed by the doctor. How quickly you can register the death and receive the death certificate will depend on which Registrar's office you visit. If you are experiencing any personal difficulties which have caused the formal process of registration to be delayed, you should contact the Registrar to explain this as soon as possible.

 ### Registration in England & Wales, and Northern Ireland

Who can register the death?

If the person died in a house or hospital (including a hospice), the death can be registered by:

*   A relative who was present at the time of death

*   A relative who had been visiting the person during the deceased's last illness

*   A relative living in the same local district

*   A person who was present at the time of death

*   A nominated person (solicitor or an executor)

This person is called **the informant**.

If the person did not die in a house or hospital, the death can be registered by:

*   Any relative able to provide the information required by the Registrar (see the following page)

*   Any person present at the time of death

*   The person who found the body

*   The person responsible for the body

*   The person responsible for the funeral arrangements

If the death has been reported to the Coroner

In these circumstances the Coroner informs the Registrar about the death, so no one has to attend the Registrar's office. But you will have to contact the Registrar in order to arrange for the Registrar to give you (or send you) the death certificate.

Where can you register the death?

- If it is convenient, you can register the death with the Registrar of Births, Deaths and Marriages for the Sub-District of the Registrar's office where the death occurred. This Registrar is called the '**Receiving Registrar**'.

- If it is not convenient, then the death can be registered by attending another Registrar's office called the '**Attesting Registrar**', which may be nearer to you. The Attesting Registrar will then inform the Registrar mentioned above, but you will need to allow additional time before the certificates can be issued.

You can find out the location of the most convenient Registrar's office in England & Wales by accessing www.gro.gov.uk or by telephoning 0151 471 4805.

It is wise to phone for an appointment (or to ask a friend to do this for you). The Registrar and his or her staff will make every effort to deal sensitively with you as a bereaved person, and they would like to make sure that the time you need is set aside.

What documents do you, as the informant, need to take to the Registrar's office?

- The medical certificate of the cause of death (please note that if the medical certificate is taken to the Attesting Registrar, then that Registrar will send the medical certificate and other information to the Receiving Registrar).

- Any forms that you have been given by the Coroner if the death has been referred to the Coroner.

What information do you need to give the Registrar about the person who has died?

- Date and place of birth.

- First names and surname (and previous surname if applicable).

- Last address (if the death was away from the normal home, then the normal home address should be given, rather than the address where the death occurred).

- Date and place of death.

- Name, occupation and date of birth of any surviving widow/widower/civil partner.

- Whether the person was receiving a pension or allowance from public funds.

If there are no queries, the Registrar then makes an entry of the death and gives you the documents below.

What documents will the Registrar give you?

- A green Certificate for Burial or Cremation. You can give this certificate to the funeral director or to any other person arranging the funeral. This certificate is part of the authorisation process for the burial or cremation.

- If the Coroner is involved and has authorised a post-mortem examination, then only the Coroner can authorise the cremation or burial.

- A death certificate. (You may want to consider requesting more than one copy as you will probably need to send the certificate to various financial institutions, such as banks and building societies. Although these copies have to be paid for, it may be wise to err on the side of caution when counting how many copies you think you need – most people find that there are several organisations which require them, and photocopies are not generally accepted.)

- A white Certificate of Registration of Death (Form BD8), which you then complete and send to your local Department of Social Security office or Jobcentre Plus office. On this form you state whether you might be entitled to state bereavement benefits. If you are entitled to benefits, then the Social Security office or Jobcentre Plus office will send you a BB1 Claim Form – the form for bereavement benefits. (This form, as well as notes on filling it in, can be downloaded from the web enablement section of Lawpack's website – see page 4 on how to register).

If you need more information on registering a death, the Department for Work and Pensions (DWP) produces a useful booklet, '*What to Do After a Death in England and Wales*,' which can be downloaded from the web enablement section of Lawpack's website (see page 4 on how to register).

Stillbirths

A stillbirth occurs when a baby has been born dead after the 24th week of pregnancy. The birth and death must both be registered, but 42 days is allowed for this to be done, and both are registered in a single process. The mother and father and the occupier of the premises where the stillbirth occurred are the people able to register the stillborn child.

A doctor or certified midwife who was present at the birth would be able to issue a medical certificate of stillbirth, stating the cause of death and the duration of the pregnancy.

If no doctor or midwife was present at the birth, then the mother, or anyone else who was present, would need to fill out Form 35, available from the Registrar of Births and Deaths, stating that he or she believed that the baby had been stillborn.

If it is not certain that the child was stillborn, the case may be reported to the Coroner who may then order a post-mortem or an inquest. The Coroner will issue a certificate of the cause of death when the inquiry is complete.

When registering a stillbirth you must provide the following information to the Registrar:

- Name and residence of the mother and father

- Name of the child

A copy of the stillborn birth registration is free of charge, if requested, and there is a charge for the death certificate. Once the death certificate has been issued, the baby's funeral may be arranged.

Miscarriages

Some babies die before the 24th week of pregnancy. If the miscarriage occurred in hospital, the hospital should offer, as a minimum, a respectful means of dealing with the foetus. Some will offer a simple ceremony led by the hospital chaplain.

If you have lost a child in this way, and would like to arrange a funeral, a medical certificate will be needed for burial or cremation. The majority of crematoriums make minimal charges for funerals of stillborn or miscarried children and many funeral directors carry out a service free of charge.

 ## Registration in Scotland

Where can you register the death?

Deaths and stillbirths which occur in Scotland may be registered at the office of any local Registrar. You can find out the location of the most convenient Registrar's office in Scotland by accessing the website www.gro-scotland.gov.uk or by contacting telephone enquiries.

Who can register the death?

The people who may inform the Registrar are as follows:

- Any relative of the person who has died
- Any person present at the death
- The executor or other legal representative of the person who has died
- The occupier of the premises where the death took place
- Any person having knowledge of the particulars to be registered

What documents do you, as the informant, need to take to the Registrar's office?

The Registrar will request the medical certificate of the cause of death. If this is not available, then the Registrar will request the name and address of a doctor who can be asked to give the certificate.

You should try to take with you:

- The medical certificate of the cause of death
- The birth certificate of the person who has died
- His or her marriage certificate (if applicable)

- A medical card of the person who has died

- Documents relating to the deceased's pension or benefits (if applicable)

If you are unable to locate these documents, this will not prevent the registration of the death.

Stillbirths

Any stillbirth which occurs in Scotland must be registered within 21 days, in any registration district in Scotland.

A doctor or midwife must produce for the Registrar a certificate of stillbirth. If there is no certificate of stillbirth, an informant must make a declaration on a special form called Form 7, which is obtainable from the Registrar. The case is then referred to the Procurator Fiscal (a person who is equivalent to a Coroner in England & Wales), who notifies the Registrar General of the results of his or her investigations.

For a cremation, a certificate of stillbirth must be given by the doctor who was in attendance at the confinement or who conducted the post-mortem. Before a cremation can take place the death must be registered. Registration is the responsibility of a parent of the stillborn child, but it can be done by another relative who is aware of the circumstances, by the occupier of the premises where the stillbirth took place, or by any person present at the stillbirth.

Certificate of registration

From 1 January 2007, local Registrars in Scotland have been able to issue an abbreviated Extract of Death, which is free of charge, although a charge is made for additional copies. The abbreviated Extract is suitable for notification purposes only in circumstances where the cause of death is not relevant. The website of the General Register Office in Scotland (www.gro-scotland.gov.uk) states that the Abbreviated Extract should be sufficient to close a bank account of the person who has died. However, a full Extract of Death would most likely be needed by an insurance company.

For other purposes and, in particular, for burial or cremation, Form 14, a Certificate of Registration of Death, is required. This is issued by the Registrar on receipt of Form 11, which is the doctor's certificate of the cause of death.

The Registrar also gives the informant a Registration or Notification of Death Form, which can be used for National Insurance and Social Security purposes.

The Scottish Executive (www.scotland.gov.uk) produces a useful booklet, '*What to Do After a Death in Scotland: Practical Advice for Times of Bereavement*', which can be downloaded from the web enablement section of Lawpack's website (see page 4 on how to register).

Deaths abroad

If a British person has died abroad, the registration of his or her death must be in the country where he or she has died and the country's relevant authority should issue the death certificate. In order that there are no subsequent problems with the funeral or probate ('probate' meaning the administration of the dead person's financial affairs), the death should be registered with the British Consul in order to create a record of the death in the UK. The death certificate should be sent to the Foreign and Commonwealth Office.

Procedures vary and it is wise to check with the Foreign and Commonwealth Office to ensure that the correct information is available. A fee is payable for the process and for each certificate issued at registration.

If the body should have been repatriated without a death certificate, application should be made to the Foreign and Commonwealth Office for a consular death certificate at the following address:

Foreign and Commonwealth Office
Nationality and Passport Section
Room G/35, Old Admiralty Building
London SW1P 2PA
Tel: 020 7008 0186 (open 10am till noon)
Email: BMDenquiries@fco.gov.uk
Website: www.fco.gov.uk

If the death was sudden or unexplained, then in certain circumstances the death will have to be referred to the Coroner in the UK. The Coroner will review the evidence available and decide whether to hold an inquest (see page 22).

Deaths in the armed forces

When a death of a member of the armed forces occurs abroad, the Ministry of Defence (MOD) allows the next of kin one of two choices:

1. A funeral overseas, including all costs and allowing two people from the UK to attend.

2. Repatriation of the body, where it is practical, at public expense to a funeral director in the UK of the family's choice. When the body has reached the funeral director the family becomes responsible. The MOD provides the coffin and a grant of up to £1,309 towards burial or £700 towards cremation (figures as at February 2007). To find out the latest figures, you can call the Service Personnel and Veterans Agency on 0800 169 2277 for more information.

If a serviceman or woman dies in the UK, the next of kin has three choices:

1. A military funeral at public expense arranged and paid for by the MOD.

2. A private funeral with limited military assistance. The MOD will pay for the coffin and transport of the body from the place of death to a funeral director chosen by the family.

3. A private expense funeral. This is where the next of kin will arrange for the body to be collected and he or she will make arrangements for the funeral privately. The MOD will provide some financial assistance for the burial or cremation.

A person who has died while serving in the armed forces may be buried in a military cemetery. This burial will be arranged at public expense if there is a military cemetery near to where the death occurred.

If someone has died while receiving a war disablement pension and died as a result of the disablement or was drawing an Attendance Allowance, the Department for Work and Pensions (DWP) may pay for a simple funeral. Before any formal arrangements are made the next of kin should contact the Veterans Agency (www.veteransagency.org.uk; tel. 0800 169 2277).

Organ donation

Many bereaved people derive comfort from knowing that the kidneys, corneas or any other donation from their loved one will save another life or bring improved quality of life to someone else.

The usual procedure is for the hospital to approach the next of kin to make sure that he or she does not object to organ donation. If the death was in a hospital or similar institution, the head of that institution is lawfully in possession of the body. He or she may honour the decision of the person who has died, communicated in writing or orally before two witnesses, for the body to be given for medical research, if there is no reason to think that the request has been withdrawn.

If the death has to be reported to the Coroner, the Coroner's consent may be necessary before the organs or body can be donated. A medical certificate may be issued before any organs can be removed or the body used.

All procedures relating to organ donation, the retention of organs after a post-mortem and the donation of bodies for medical research are regulated by the Human Tissue Authority:

Human Tissue Authority
Finlaison House
15–17 Furnival Street
London EC4A 1AB
Tel: 020 7211 3400
Email: enquiries@hta.gov.uk
Website: www.hta.gov.uk

If a body is to be used for teaching purposes, then the body may be kept for up to three years. The medical school will let the relatives know when the body is available for a funeral. The relatives may arrange and pay for the funeral or the medical school will arrange and pay for a simple funeral.

Information on funerals, post-mortems and inquests is provided later in this Kit.

Post-mortems and inquests

This section is designed to explain about post-mortems and also to help you if the death of your loved one has been referred to the Coroner.

Post-mortems

A post-mortem (also called an 'autopsy') is an examination of the body after death to determine the cause of death, or to obtain other important information. A post-mortem may take place if it is ordered by the Coroner (in England & Wales, and Northern Ireland) or the Procurator Fiscal (in Scotland), or if it is consented to by an individual before he or she died, or if it has been agreed to by relatives after the death.

In England & Wales, and Northern Ireland, the Human Tissue Authority Code of Practice for Post-Mortem Examination (Code 3 July 2006) makes it clear that Coroners, their Officers and hospital staff are expected to deal sensitively with bereaved people. It also sets out your rights in respect of a post-mortem examination. In Scotland, such provisions are regulated by the Human Tissue (Scotland) Act 2006. Its provisions are very similar to those of the Human Tissue Authority Code of Practice, and the Human Tissue Authority carries out some tasks on behalf of the Scottish Executive.

For people from some religious traditions, the idea of a post-mortem is difficult, especially if there is a tradition of the burial taking place very soon after death. If this is true for you, then you should seek to explain your difficulty to the Coroner/Procurator Fiscal, or with his or her Officer. It may not be possible to resolve it, but you should be dealt with sensitively and your views respected.

Hospital post-mortems

A 'consented' post-mortem is a post-mortem examination at a hospital and can only be carried out with the written consent of the relatives, the prior consent of the person who has died, or the consent of a nominated representative appointed by the person before he or she died. If a child has died, prior consent given by the child will be valid if the child was deemed competent to give it. Should this not be the case, then a decision will be sought from the adult with care responsibilities.

As a relative or other person close to the person who has died, you do not have the right to override any prior decision about the post-mortem your relative made before he or she died, although the hospital staff will discuss the matter with you. Where consent has not been given by a nominated representative appointed by the person who has died, or by the deceased before his or her death, the people who may give consent for the post-mortem after the death are those in a 'qualifying relationship'. The list below gives the relationships involved; the list is ordered to show who will be approached first; relationships lower down the list will qualify only if there is no other appropriate person available.

Consent to a hospital post-mortem – qualifying relationships

- Spouse or partner (including civil or same sex partner)

- Parent or child

- Brother or sister

- Grandparent or grandchild

- Niece or nephew

- Stepfather or stepmother

- Half-brother or half-sister

- Friend of long standing

If there is a disagreement between family members, you should try to discuss the matter with the hospital staff involved. It may not be possible to reach agreement, but it may avoid later problems if everyone has a chance to receive information and state their points of view.

 ## Dealing with the body – organ donation for research and transplantation

If the person who has died wanted his or her body or specific organs to be donated for medical research, this is valid, provided that it has been recorded in writing and witnessed. A surviving relative does not have the legal right to override this decision, although if you object, you should try to discuss your objections with the clinician involved.

The same proviso applies to the known wishes of the person who has died (or his or her nominated representative) in the case of organ donation for transplantation. In both cases, if no nominated representative for this purpose exists, the list of those from whom consent may be sought is identical to the list applying to post-mortems – see above.

All matters relating to post-mortems, organ and tissue retention and donation are set out in detail in the Codes of Practice of the Human Tissue Authority.

 ## The role of the Coroner

The duty of the Coroner is to determine the cause of death. Amongst the cases which may be referred to the Coroner are those where it appears that the death may have been violent, or unnatural, or due to suicide or accident, or those where the death occurred in custody, or where no doctor saw the person within 14 days of death. Once a death has been reported to the Coroner, it may not be registered, or the funeral held, until the Coroner gives authority for this.

Some of the information in this section is based on a Model Charter for Coroners, issued by the Department for Constitutional Affairs. There will be variations in the way that the Charter is implemented by each local Coroner.

The Coroner's post-mortems

A post-mortem may not be required if the Coroner is satisfied that a doctor is able to confirm that the death was from natural causes. Of the deaths reported to the Coroner, about half result in a post-mortem examination being used to establish the cause of death. This is carried out by a pathologist.

The Coroner should hold details of the immediate next of kin of the person who has died, and should notify that person of the decision to hold a post-mortem and the reason(s) why it is needed. You have a right to be represented at the post-mortem by a doctor, but you need to be aware that post-mortems normally need to be carried out as soon as possible, so there may be limits to the notice you will receive. A charge will be payable if a doctor attends on your behalf. You may request a copy of the post-mortem report. As this will be a medical report, and may be distressing, you may wish to ask your GP (or the doctor attending the post-mortem on your behalf) to explain it to you. There may be a charge for the report.

If the post-mortem shows that the death was due to natural causes, then the Coroner will send Pink Form B (Form 100), which gives the cause of death, to the Registrar of Deaths, and at this point the death can be registered by the relatives and a Certificate of Burial can be issued by the Registrar. If the body is to be cremated rather than buried, the Certificate for Cremation, called Form E, will be issued by the Coroner.

As a bereaved person you do not have the right to refuse a post-mortem examination ordered by the Coroner. However, the procedures should be explained to you and before the post-mortem is carried out, the Coroner should inform you whether any organs or tissue will be kept after the examination, for how long the material needs to be kept, and the options for dealing with it when the Coroner no longer requires it. This information may affect your decisions about the timing of the funeral. Experience has also shown that some families wish to have an appropriate, separate ceremony for dealing respectfully with organs and tissues, in situations where these have been released by the Coroner, when a funeral has already taken place.

If, after the post-mortem, the Coroner is satisfied as to the cause of death, then the body may be released for burial or cremation.

Scotland: the Procurator Fiscal

There are no Coroners in Scotland; the relevant officer is the Procurator Fiscal, who has a responsibility to investigate all unexpected and unexplained deaths.

The Procurator Fiscal may enquire into any death brought to his or her notice, and anyone who has concerns about a death may report it to him or her.

The Procurator Fiscal may order a post-mortem examination, for which the consent of relatives is not required. When the investigations are complete, the Procurator Fiscal may hold a Fatal Accident Enquiry where there are issues of public safety or matters of general public concern, or where there is a need to highlight the circumstances which led to the death. A Fatal Accident Enquiry must be held if the death occurred during employment or while the deceased was in legal custody. The Fatal Accident Enquiry is held in public. Its functions are similar to those of an inquest in England & Wales – see below.

Some deaths reported to the Procurator Fiscal will result in a criminal investigation and/or prosecution.

The Victim Information and Advice Service (www.crownoffice.gov.uk/Victims; tel: 0131 226 2626) is available to help bereaved relatives where the Procurator Fiscal is involved in investigating a death.

Inquests

If an inquest is to be held in England & Wales, and Northern Ireland, the Coroner must inform:

- the married or civil partner of the person who has died;

- the nearest relative (if different); and

- the personal representative (if different); for example, the executor or administrator of the estate of the person who has died.

If an inquest is going to occur, the Coroner will normally allow the burial or cremation once an examination of the body has been completed. However, if someone has been charged with an offence in connection with the death, there may be delays in order to obtain evidence and because the defence has the right to request an additional post-mortem examination. In such cases, the inquest will be opened and adjourned pending the result of the court case. The Coroner may provide an interim certificate of the fact of death so as to assist the personal representatives in looking after the estate.

 ### Role of the inquest

The inquest is a fact-finding inquiry to find out:

- Who has died

- When and where the death occurred

- How the cause of death arose

The inquest is not a trial and does not find out who may have been to blame for the death under criminal law, or who may be held liable in civil law. However, the Coroner, in addition to determining the cause of death, may investigate 'any acts or omissions which directly led to the cause of death'. Where court proceedings are applicable, they will take place after the inquest.

What happens at an inquest?

- The Coroner has the authority to identify and summon witnesses to give evidence.

- A person wanting to give evidence or question a witness should inform the Coroner as soon as possible after the death.

- All evidence is given under oath.

- Anyone who has a 'proper interest' may themselves, or through a lawyer, question a witness at the inquest.

- In cases involving criminal proceedings, or in other circumstances where there is likely to be a delay in being able to complete the inquest, the Coroner may issue an interim death certificate.

- For some inquests there may be a jury (e.g. where death may have been caused by an industrial accident or the death occurred in police custody or in prison).

- When an inquest has been completed, a person who has a proper interest in the inquest may apply to see the notes written by the Coroner during or after the inquest or may have a copy of the notes on the payment of a fee.

- Legal aid is not normally available for providing representation at an inquest.

 ## Possible verdicts

There is no requirement for verdicts to be in a set form. Some Coroners are now using the narrative verdict, which is a short summary of the circumstances of the death and may illustrate contributory factors. Other verdicts often used are:

- Natural causes

- Accident/misadventure

- Suicide

- Death from drug use

- Unlawful or lawful killing

- Industrial disease

- Neglect

- Open verdicts (where there is insufficient evidence for any other verdict)

 ## Inquests and bereavement

There is no doubt that the prospect of a formal public hearing into the death is a source of pressure and anxiety for many bereaved people. A balancing factor is likely to be that you will want to know the truth about how the person died and that you hope that the inquest will help to establish this; however, as the inquest cannot identify responsibility for the death, it will not provide the full answer in every case. You may not agree with the verdict, but you will need to bear in mind that the inquest may not be the end of the process; for example, a verdict of accidental death does not preclude a claim for damages or a possible prosecution.

 ## Dealing with the media

Inquests are public hearings and the press may be present. Some cases attract more press attention than others and it is not always easy to predict when the media will turn up. Bereaved families are sometimes hurt and angry if they feel that press coverage is misleading. On the other hand, being able to tell your story to a responsible journalist can be helpful. You may want to enlist the help of someone else if the press attention is intrusive (a friend, perhaps, or a police officer if the death is being investigated). If you feel that you have grounds for complaint against anyone from the media, you may wish to contact the programme maker or broadcasting channel, or newspaper, or the Press Complaints Commission (www.pcc.org.uk) for newspapers, or Ofcom (www.ofcom.org.uk) for broadcasters.

 ## Should family members attend?

If you are called as a witness, you will have to attend. Many bereaved people who are not witnesses do attend the inquest and some put their questions forward. No one should feel, however, that they must go if they consider it to be too distressing. It is a good idea to discuss the matter so that the situation of each family member affected can be dealt with; perhaps, for example, those who do not wish to attend or are not able to do so could be told what has happened by other family members after the hearing.

 ## The Coroner's other responsibilities

- If the death has been referred to the Coroner, then the Coroner must agree to the removal of any organs for transplantation.

- In all cases (i.e. whether or not the death has been referred to the Coroner) where the body is to be taken out of England & Wales (or Northern Ireland), the Coroner must agree. Four clear days should be allowed for the Coroner's reply, unless written permission is obtained sooner.

- Where the body has been brought from abroad, the Coroner may be able to give some help in finding out the cause of death and he or she may be required to hold an inquest.

 ## Getting help

The inquest may bring up many issues and feelings for you; listed in the 'Useful contacts' section of this Kit are organisations able to help – see page 46.

If the death is the subject of a police investigation, the police will normally designate a Police Family Liaison Officer to help you.

Funerals

After the death of someone close, the funeral should be a source of comfort and an opportunity to celebrate the person's life. Arranging a funeral is therefore an important responsibility, which will be influenced by the wishes and beliefs of the person who has died, and of those who are left.

The funeral is normally arranged by the executor of the estate (i.e. the person appointed in a Will to carry out the wishes of the person who has died), by the next of kin, or someone else who has offered to take responsibility for it. Before you make the arrangements, it is wise to check on the finance available, as the person who makes the arrangements will normally receive all bills.

If you are making the funeral arrangements, you may be aware of the wishes of the person who has died. Sometimes these are expressed in a Will, or in the advance purchase of a funeral plan, or they may simply have been made known to family and friends. They are not legally binding, but clearly you would need good reason for doing otherwise.

A good first step is to decide whether to use a funeral director, but, of course, this is a matter of personal preference. If you do not use a funeral director, you may incur lower costs, but you will have greater responsibility for co-ordinating the arrangements at a difficult time.

First choices

- Whether to use a funeral director and, if one is engaged, choosing one.
- What type of ceremony to have – whether it is religious or non-religious, or will have a mixture of content.
- Where the ceremony will be held.
- Whether it will be cremation or burial.
- How much to spend.
- How to pay for the funeral.
- Whether to have a gathering for friends and family afterwards, and in what form.

It is probably wise to start the preliminary enquiries as soon as you feel able to do so, but remember that the death must have been registered (or, if the Coroner (in England & Wales, and Northern Ireland) or the Procurator Fiscal (in Scotland) is involved, he must have given authorisation) before the funeral may take place.

Finding a funeral director

You may know of a funeral director you can trust because you have previously used their service, or you may have a recommendation from family or friends. If you do not, then a good place to start is with a trade association, such as:

* The National Association of Funeral Directors – www.nafd.org.uk

* The Society of Allied and Independent Funeral Directors – www.saif.org.uk

Both have searchable websites enabling you to find funeral directors in your area and they both maintain a Code of Practice and complaints procedure with which member firms are expected to comply.

You can also contact your local Citizens' Advice Bureau (CAB) or your local council's Trading Standards Department for advice if you are unhappy with the funeral director's service.

What you should expect from a funeral director

A good funeral director should provide you with advice and support, and should be able to make suggestions for you in line with your choices and preferences. A written quotation of the costs should be provided. Here is an outline of the basic service you should expect from a funeral director.

* The transfer of the body from the hospital or place of death to the funeral director's premises/chapel of rest or to a family member's home if that is preferred.

* Arrangements to view the body while it is on the funeral director's premises.

* Care of the body and the carrying out of your wishes for clothes or jewellery to be worn, for example.

* Familiarity with local facilities for burial or cremation, and respect for your wishes concerning other possible options, such as a green burial (see page 27).

* Arrangements for the burial or cremation, including providing the appropriate documentation to the cemetery or cremation authority.

* Sympathetic explanation of any issues which may be difficult, such as precautions against infection which are needed if the person died from HIV/Aids or some other infectious conditions. (This may mean that embalming is not possible, which may affect the possibility of viewing the body.)

* Knowledge of the range of local faith representatives across all communities and faiths, and advice on how to carry out your wishes in respect of any ceremonies which are required.

* A clear indication of the costs involved, for example:
  * Embalming
  * The cost of the funeral service and/or cremation
  * The coffin
  * Grave fees and cemetery charges

- Transport

Where funeral arrangements are sold as a package, make sure that it is explained to you what is included. If you wish to arrange newspaper announcements and to have a printed order of service, you will need to allow for these costs and you may also wish to order flowers.

In addition to satisfying yourself as to the costs incurred, it is wise to be clear about when payment is due, in case you need to arrange finance to cover this.

Green funerals, woodland burials and home burials

Expectations of funerals and burials are changing all the time. At the time of writing this Kit there are over 200 natural burial sites in the UK, and a number of suppliers of environmentally friendly coffins. The Natural Death Centre (www.naturaldeath. org.uk) is able to provide advice and information.

It is also possible to bury your loved one at home, provided that conditions designed to protect groundwater and surface water can be met. In order to meet these, you should contact the Environmental Health Department of your local authority.

Burial at sea

There are very few places around the UK coast where this is permitted, and it is not allowed when the body has been embalmed. Burial at sea requires a licence, for which an application should be made to the Marine Consents and Environment Unit at the Department for the Environment, Food and Rural Affairs (www.defra.gov.uk).

Designing a funeral ceremony

Whether the ceremony is to be secular or religious, the points below are outlined to help you think about how you want to organise the occasion. It is worth considering the following:

- **Would you like to have a celebrant (someone who leads the proceedings)?**
  Ministers of religion often perform this function, but it can by done by anyone, or shared between two or three people. As well as trying to ensure that everything is dignified and goes smoothly, it is worth considering who can best shoulder this responsibility for you, if you are likely to find the day very distressing. In addition to ministers of religion, the Institute of Civil Funerals (www.iocf.org.uk) and the British Humanist Association (www.humanism. org.uk) will be able to help you find a celebrant.

- **How long do you need for the ceremony?**
  Although we would like to think that bereaved people's feelings are always considered, some crematoriums are still booked in half-hour slots, so do make sure that your ceremony is designed for the length of time available, as a feeling of rush can be very distressing.

- **Would you like someone to speak about the life of the person who has died?**

  At www.co-operativefuneralcare.co.uk, you will find '*Well Chosen Words, How to Write a Eulogy*', with a foreword by the Poet Laureate, Andrew Motion, which may be able to help you.

- **Should your child attend the funeral?**

  You, with your child, will need to find your own right answer to this question; there are no rules. The most important thing you can do is to explain to your child what is happening, in terms appropriate to his or her age, to answer questions as honestly as you can, and to respect your child's wishes if possible. If you are likely to be very distressed yourself, and your child wishes to attend, it may be appropriate to find another trusted family member or friend to look after your child during the ceremony. There are many ways in which children may be helped to take part; for example, by writing a letter which may be placed in the coffin, or by writing his or her own message on the label of some flowers. Older children may wish to join in by speaking about the person who has died; this may be helpful, although no pressure should be placed upon them to do this.

- **Do you want to have flowers or donations?**

  People who attend the funeral will want to support you by providing the right kind of tribute, so it is a good idea to specify, for example, whether you want to have flowers, whether you would like family flowers only, or whether you would like donations to one or more charities. If you employ a funeral director, the firm will be able to handle flowers and donations, if you so wish.

- **Who would you like to attend?**

  Where there are several stages to a ceremony (e.g. a cremation followed by a burial of the ashes or a funeral service followed by burial in a cemetery) it is worthwhile thinking about who you would like to attend each part of the ceremony and to get someone to pay great attention to transport arrangements for you. The roadways in some cemeteries can become congested and this can be distressing.

Arranging a cremation

 ### Documents required for a cremation

Before a cremation may take place, additional evidence of the cause of death is required, provided by an independent doctor; a fee is payable for this. You will need:

- Form A, which is the application for cremation. It is completed by the next of kin or executor. It must be countersigned by a householder who knows the person. Some crematoriums will let the funeral director countersign the form.

- Form B, the medical certificate of the cause of death, signed by the GP or hospital doctor.

- Form C, signed by a second, independent doctor. (A fee is payable.)

- Form F, the crematorium certificate, signed by the local medical referee at the crematorium, after he or she has checked Forms B and C to ensure that all the requirements have been met.

- The green certificate, which is the Certificate for Cremation, issued by the Registrar of Deaths.

- A Service Details Form, which you use to inform the crematorium about the funeral service.

If the Coroner (in England & Wales, and Northern Ireland) or the Procurator Fiscal (in Scotland) is involved, then he issues Form E, a Certificate for Cremation, so Forms B and C are not required.

 ## Decisions about the ashes after a cremation

The person who has died may have expressed his or her wishes about where he or she wants the ashes to be scattered immediately after the cremation or later. Ashes may be scattered in many places, including the crematorium where the funeral has been held or, for example, they can be buried in a churchyard or cemetery or woodland site. Ashes may also be scattered at sea; this does not require a licence and there are a number of ferry companies which have well established local services for this purpose.

Some people who have died request that their ashes are not scattered but are retained by the family. If you have engaged a funeral director, he or she will be able to help you with any questions you may have.

If your tradition involves casting the ashes into a river or stream, this is perfectly possible, provided that you follow some basic guidance about the choice of site and that you avoid placing other items into the water, such as wreaths, particularly if these have plastic or metal attachments. A helpful leaflet '*Funeral Practices, Spreading Ashes and Caring for the Environment*' is available from the Environment Agency (email: enquiries@environment-agency.gov.uk; tel: 0870 850 6506 (Monday to Friday, 8am–6pm)).

If, during the deceased's lifetime, he or she had benefited from a replacement joint, after cremation there will be a residual amount of the high grade cobalt steel used to make the joint. Crematoriums, which are members of a recycling scheme run by the Institute of Cemetery and Crematorium Management, collect this material for recycling, with most of the high grade material being used by a specialist company to make new orthopaedic implants. Other remaining metals are used in traditional recycling. At crematoriums where this scheme is in operation, the consent of the appropriate relative will be sought.

At the time of writing this Kit, over 100,000 bereaved families have consented to the recycling scheme and the funds raised have been distributed to charities. Further information is available at www.iccm-uk.com.

Arranging a burial

 ## Documents required for a burial

- For all burials you will need the Registrar's green Certificate for Burial or the Coroner's (or the Procurator Fiscal's) order for burial if the death was referred to him or her.

- If the burial is going to take place in a cemetery, then you will need to complete the cemetery's paperwork. If the cemetery is a municipal cemetery, then apply to them. If the cemetery is a churchyard, then apply to the member of clergy responsible for that parish who will inform you about the procedure. In either case if there is already a grave plot available, you may find details of the title deeds with the Will or other papers of the person who has died.

- If the burial will take place at a woodland site, then contact the Natural Death Centre (www.naturaldeath.org.uk; tel: 0871 288 2098).

Funeral costs

Funeral costs vary according to location and between different providers. The 2006 Survey of Funeral Costs, which was commissioned by insurers American Life, estimated the average price of a burial in the UK as £2,363 and the average price of a cremation as £1,973, not including non-essential costs. In this context, non-essential costs were defined as flowers, catering, a newspaper death notice, printed order of service cards and headstones or other memorials.

 ### Paying for the funeral

Possible sources of funds may be:

- A funeral pre-payment plan

- The estate of the person who has died

- Family and friends

- A trade union or professional body

- A life insurance policy

- A bereavement payment paid by the government (only payable to those under retirement age)

- A pension scheme, but this will depend on the rules of the particular scheme

- The Social Fund (this will be a loan) – see below for more information.

In cases where no relatives are able to pay for the funeral, either the hospital where the death occurred, or the local authority, may take responsibility for arranging a simple funeral.

The Social Fund

You can make a claim for a loan from the Social Fund by applying to Jobcentre Plus, but there are various qualification criteria:

1. You or your partner must be receiving one of the following payments or allowances from the government:

   - Income-Based Jobseeker's Allowance

- Working Tax Credit where there is a disabled worker credit in the benefit
- Child Tax Credit where it is at a rate higher than the family element rate
- Council Tax Credit
- Income Support
- Housing Benefit
- Pension Credit

2. It must have been reasonable (in the opinion of the agency paying the benefit) for you to pay for the funeral.

3. The funeral is in the UK and the person who has died normally lived in the UK.

It is also worth bearing in mind the following points:

1. If the person who has died has no partner, then someone else may attempt to claim the Social Fund payment.

2. If the funeral takes place elsewhere in the European Union or in Switzerland, it may be possible to receive a payment from the Social Fund, but the amount will be based on UK costs.

A Social Fund payment may not cover all the funeral costs incurred because the assessment of the payment (before the various deductions (see below)) is based on providing a 'simple, respectful, low-cost funeral, normally within the UK'.

Deductions will be made for the following:

- Any assets of the person who has died which are available to you or to your partner
- Any lump sum that is available to pay for the funeral costs
- Any contributions to the costs (e.g. from a charity or a relative)
- Any funeral grant under the war pension provisions, if the person who died was a war pensioner

Even if you receive a payment from the Social Fund, you will have to pay back the payment from the estate of the deceased person. The estate includes any money, property and other assets, but does not include any house or personal possessions that are left to a widow, widower or surviving civil partner.

If you would like more information on the Social Fund, you can download the government's leaflet '*Help with Funeral Expenses from the Social Fund*', as well as Claim Form SF200 and its notes, from the web enablement section of Lawpack's website (see page 4 on how to register).

After the funeral

Many people arrange a social gathering of some kind. This enables those who have been bereaved to benefit from the comfort of family or friends, and provides an opportunity for them to exchange memories of the person who has died.

Cost, convenience, the amount of work involved and how much help you have are factors which will help you decide whether to have a gathering, and where to hold it.

In the days immediately following, your reactions and preoccupations will vary according to your individual situation. You may not know beforehand how you will feel about going back to work, whether you want the company of family and friends, or whether you need time alone. The period immediately following a death is a demanding time; take each day one at a time, and do what you can to look after yourself and those close to you.

Memorials

If you wish to have a headstone or other memorial on a grave, you have time to consider your choice as this cannot be installed immediately after burial. This is an opportunity to consider whether there is anyone else with whom you would like to discuss the choice of memorial. The National Association of Memorial Masons has a searchable website (www.namm.co.uk) to help you find a local Memorial Mason. Members are required to follow a Code of Business Working Practices. You should also check with the management of the burial ground (whether this is the local authority or a religious body) as there are usually stipulations about the kind of memorials which may be used, and it is best to know this in advance.

 ## Virtual memorials

Web-based memorials are becoming very popular; an internet search will reveal a choice of several. Depending on the configuration of the site, pictures, music, poetry and other verbal tributes may be possible. Before making your choice it is wise to:

- Look at the site on several different occasions so that you know that it is properly maintained and easily accessible.

- Make sure that you can tell:

    - Who is running the site? Is it a charity or a commercial company?

    - Does it carry advertising and is this acceptable to you?

- What does it cost? How long will your memorial be left in place, and what are the renewal fees?

- Does the site carry user feedback? How recent is this?

- How easy is it to understand the user instructions?

- Who will be able to access any pages you create?

A good memorial site can be a great help, in that it will allow several bereaved people to make a tribute and to share it with others if they wish to do so.

Finance and property

After someone has died, arrangements will need to be made to deal with his or her money and property and to make provision for anyone affected by the death. You may be reading this because you have lost someone very close and are having to cope with all the practicalities as well as your grief, or perhaps you are less closely affected but are trying to help a friend. One of the aims of this Kit is to help you with the basic essential tasks to meet your own needs, to comply with the law and to follow the wishes of the person who has died.

There are often a lot of legal and administrative procedures, such as registering the death, possibly dealing with an inquest, the funeral and burial or cremation and then dealing with various organisations (e.g. the Department for Work and Pensions, Jobcentre Plus, banks, building societies and insurance companies). Here are some helpful tips on how to deal with the administrative paperwork:

- If the task seems overwhelming, it may be worthwhile to enlist the help of a friend or family member.

- Read the paperwork carefully and ask for help if you are unsure.

- Keep a copy of the paperwork and documentation you send to organisations. Only send original documents where required, otherwise use copies.

- Be aware of the time limits where these are specified.

State benefits

- If the person who has died was receiving a state benefit, you need to notify the Department for Work and Pensions and any other relevant department of the death.

- If the person who has died and you, as his or her surviving husband, wife or civil partner (called the 'survivor' in the paragraphs later in this Kit), were both receiving the basic state pension when your partner died, then in some circumstances you may be able to use the National Insurance contributions from the person who has died to get extra basic state pension. For further information, contact the Department for Work and Pensions.

- If the person who has died was receiving a State Earnings Related Pension Scheme (called a 'SERPS' pension), then you, as the 'survivor', may inherit some or all of the SERPS pension of the person who has died.

- If your partner has died, your financial circumstances will have changed with your partner's death so you may now be entitled to state benefits or have increased entitlement if you were receiving benefits prior to the death of your partner.

- You may be able to receive help with the funeral expenses from the Social Security system, called the 'Social Fund' (see page 30).

- There is also a leaflet entitled '*If you are Widowed*', obtainable from your local Jobcentre Plus (or you can download it from the web enablement section of Lawpack's website – see page 4 on how to register), which may be helpful.

The following state bereavement benefits and payments are also available:

- **Bereavement Payment**

  To receive a Bereavement Payment (which is currently £2,000) to assist with the immediate expenses after a death you, as the claimant, must be:

  - under state pension age (currently 60 for women and 65 for men); or

  - over state pension age and your late husband, wife or civil partner was not entitled to a state pension, based on his or her own contributions when he or she died.

- **Bereavement Allowance**

  This benefit may be payable to you, as a surviving widow or widower or civil partner, if you are aged 45 or over but below state pension age when your husband, wife or civil partner died.

  The amount of benefit is determined by the National Insurance contributions of your partner who has died and your age when he or she died.

  If an entitlement is established, then the amount of the allowance is dependent on your age. If you are 55 or over and less than pension age, then the full rate of the Bereavement Allowance is payable. If you are between 45 and 55, then the amount payable is less than the full rate.

  The allowance is payable from the date of death for a maximum of 52 weeks. If you, as a widow, widower or civil partner, become entitled to the state pension before the end of the 52-week period, then the Bereavement Allowance ceases.

- **Widowed Parent's Allowance**

  There are two circumstances when you may be eligible for a Widowed Parent's Allowance:

  1. If you are under pension age and receiving Child Benefit for one or more children and your deceased husband, wife or civil partner died on or after 9 April 2001; or

  2. You are expecting a child by your late husband or as the result of artificial insemination or in vitro fertilisation.

- **War Widow's Pension**

  There may be help if you are a relative a of a war pensioner. Information is available from the Veterans Agency (see www.veteransagency.org.uk).

- **Guardian's Allowance**

  You may be eligible for this allowance if you are bringing up someone else's child and are entitled to Child Benefit. Normally both the child's parents must be dead. However, there are exceptions.

For more information on benefits, if you are over pension age, contact the Pension Service on 0845 606 0265. If you are under pension age, contact Jobcentre Plus on 0845 608 8602.

Bank accounts

It is important to notify the bank/building society or any institution holding funds belonging to the person who has died as soon as possible (a template letter for this purpose can be found on page 53). The template letter outlines a range of circumstances which apply, as it is vital to notify the bank in the following circumstances:

- If the account was in the sole name of the person who has died, but you are dependent on access to it so that you can live from day to day and pay your bills. You may also need funds to pay for the funeral. Do make sure that your bank knows this, if this is the case. Banks vary in terms of the extent to which they are prepared to release funds before probate has been granted.

- If the account was in the joint names of yourself and the person who has died.

- If you have been appointed as executor in the Will of the person who has died (in which case you will normally need to open an executor's bank account).

It is also important to check immediately whether the original death certificate is required, or whether a certified copy will be accepted.

Housing

If the person who has died was in rented accommodation and a surviving relative wants to take up the tenancy, then the administrator or executor of the estate (see page 36 for more information on these roles) will need to negotiate with the landlord (council or housing society or other landlord) straight away. If the transfer of the tenancy is possible, then the appropriate documents should be requested from the landlord for signature.

If you have any queries about housing issues, you may wish to contact Shelter (www.shelter.org.uk; tel. 020 8800 4444), which has a search by area facility, or the Citizens' Advice Bureau.

If you were living with the person who has died, you may be thinking about moving after the bereavement. You may want to take some time thinking over this decision, and if the property is rented, do check your tenancy status (or ask someone to do it for you) as soon as you can.

 ### Empty house management order

An empty house management order is designed to ensure that councils are able to house people in properties that appear to be permanently empty. Inherited properties are exempt while probate is resolved, however long that takes and then for a further six months. In most cases, the property would continue to be exempt, for example, if it was sold, rented out or used as a holiday home.

Dealing with the estate

In order to deal with the money and property of the person who has died (usually referred to as his or her 'estate'), which includes identifying his or her assets, paying any debts, and making sure that the remaining money or property is correctly distributed, a legal document is required. This is called a 'Grant of Representation' (often called 'probate' in England & Wales, and Northern Ireland, or 'Confirmation' in Scotland).

The Grant of Representation will be required by many financial institutions in order to release the funds of the person who has died. It will also be required to sell or transfer a property that was not held jointly but was held in the sole name of the person who has died.

The process of obtaining the Grant involves applying to the Probate Registry, which involves providing paper information and attending an interview at a local Registry. If the person who has died has appointed one or more executors in his or her Will to deal with the estate, then they will apply for the Grant. If no executors were appointed or no Will was made, then the court, if necessary, will appoint one or more administrators to deal with the estate. Executors and administrators are also known as 'personal representatives'.

There are three types of Grant of Representation:

1. **Grant of Probate**

    If a Will has been made, it is likely that one or more executors will have been named. It is their responsibility to ensure that the wishes of the person who has died are carried out. These are often called the 'provisions' of the Will and they may concern the funeral arrangements, or the distribution of money and property. In this case, it is the executor(s) who will receive the Grant.

2. **Grant of Letters of Administration (with a Will)**

    This applies when there is a Will, but there is no executor named, or the executors are unwilling or unable to act. The Grant will be issued to the administrators.

3. **Grant of Letters of Administration**

    This applies when there is no Will or the Will is invalid and it will be issued to the administrators.

The same official forms are used for all three types of Grant of Representation.

A Grant may not be required if the estate is of a very modest value, or if the whole estate is held in joint names and passes automatically to the surviving joint owner. You may want to talk to the Probate and Inheritance Tax Helpline (0845 302 0900) or consult a solicitor to find out whether a Grant will be applicable in your particular circumstance.

 ## Applying for a Grant of Representation

You may decide to do this yourself or to use a solicitor or other service. There are a range of services offered by banks and by a number of online providers. The Law

Society (www.lawsociety.org.uk) has a searchable facility making it possible to locate a Wills and probate specialist in your area.

Even if you decide to employ a solicitor or other agent to make the application for you, leaflet PA2 '*How to Obtain Probate – A Guide for the Applicant Acting Without a Solicitor*' (available at www.hmcourts-service.gov.uk/courtfinder/forms/pa2_0206.pdf) provides a useful summary.

Who may apply for a Grant of Representation?

- The named executor in a Will.

- If there are none, or they are unable or unwilling to apply, any person named in the Will to whom the estate has been given.

- If there is no Will, the next of kin of the person who has died in the following order of priority:

  - Husband, wife or civil partner (a partnership between two people of the same sex registered according to the Civil Partnership Act 2004). Common law partners are not entitled to apply.

  - Sons or daughters, or their children, if any sons or daughters have already died. Stepchildren cannot apply.

  - Parents.

  - Brothers or sisters, or their children, if any brothers or sisters have already died.

  - Grandparents.

  - Uncles or aunts, or their children if any uncles or aunts have already died.

- Applicants must be 18 or over.

Grants of Representation in the countries of the UK

In England & Wales, the Probate Service is responsible (www. hmcourts-service. gov.uk/cms/wills.htm). For Scotland, information is available from the nearest Sheriff Court. For Northern Ireland, information may be obtained from the Probate and Matrimonial Office in Belfast on 029 072 4678, or Londonderry on 028 7136 3448.

The forms required

To obtain a Grant of Representation, you must complete various forms and send them to the Probate Registry where you want to be interviewed. A summary of the forms required in the countries of the UK is available at www.direct.gov.uk/en/RightsandResponsibilities/death/Preparation/DG_10029716.

The forms referred to in this section are those for England & Wales. These may be downloaded from the Probate Service (at www.hmcourts-service.gov.uk/cms/wills.htm) and from HM Revenue & Customs (Capital Taxes) (www.hmrc.gov.uk/cto). They are as follows:

- **PA1 – The Probate Application Form** and its Guidance Notes (PA1a) which can be obtained from your nearest Probate Registry or from the Probate and Inheritance Tax Helpline (0845 302 0900).

- **IHT205 – Short Form for Personal Applicants** and its instruction booklet (Form IHT206). IHT205 applies to estates where Inheritance Tax is unlikely in England & Wales, and Northern Ireland. In Scotland, the relevant form is Form C1.

  To complete this form, you will need a range of financial information, including:

  - Bank accounts and investments

  - Insurance policies

  - Property owned in the sole name of the person who has died

  - Debts including mortgages

  The form leads you through the process so that you can identify whether Inheritance Tax is due. If this is the case, you will need to complete **Form IHT200 (Inheritance Tax Account)** to provide the information for assessment. This form applies in all the countries of the UK.

- **Form IHT200 – Inheritance Tax Account.** If you are applying for a Grant without a solicitor, you can ask HM Revenue & Customs (Capital Taxes) to work out the tax for you.

  To get your Inheritance Tax assessed, you need to fill in Form IHT200. You must then complete Form D18 (Probate Summary), which applies in England & Wales and Northern Ireland (in Scotland, Form C1 applies). You must send Form D18 to the Probate Registry (but not Form IHT200), along with all the applicable forms (PA1) and other papers (e.g. a certified copy (not photocopy) of the death certificate, and the **original** Will) specified in the booklet PA2. The Probate Registry will then notify you of your interview date and will return Form D18 to you with your appointment letter. You then need to send Form IHT200 and Form D18, with any other documents required to HM Revenue & Customs (Capital Taxes) who will tell you whether any tax is due.

  If there is tax to pay, HM Revenue & Customs will send you a notification of the amount owed. Once you have paid the right amount of tax, HM Revenue & Customs will endorse Form D18 and return it to the Probate Registry, who will issue the Grant once you have attended an interview and your application for probate has been completed. If HM Revenue & Customs work out that there is no tax to pay, they will notify the relevant probate authority, by endorsing Form D18, and the Probate Registry will then issue the Grant once the application process has been finalised.

It is impossible to say exactly how long it may take to obtain probate. For straightforward applications, you are likely to be notified of an interview date within ten working days of receipt of your application and the interview is likely to take place within a month of your application. Your application will need to be checked (which may involve answering some questions about the information you have provided) before an interview can be arranged. The interview will provide you with an opportunity to ask questions and to confirm the accuracy of the information you have given.

The Grant of Representation will usually be given within ten days of your interview, but it is impossible to be specific about this, as circumstances vary widely. If you are using a solicitor or other agent, he or she will carry out these processes for you.

Once the Grant has been obtained, you can then show it to any person or organisation holding the deceased's property or money so that the asset can be sold, transferred or released.

The aims of the executor

The executor's (or administrator's) aims are to:

1. Identify and value the assets of the person who has died.

2. Identify the liabilities of the person who has died.

3. Distribute the legacies which are specified in the Will and then distribute the balance of the estate.

Whether or not you apply for probate, it is worth bearing in mind the following points:

- If the house is unoccupied, it should be securely locked and the house and contents insured.

- Executors should open an executor's bank account into which they will eventually deposit the proceeds of the deceased's assets and from which they will pay the bills of the person who has died.

- During the administration of the estate, the executors must keep track of every financial transaction, no matter how small.

- Once a thorough valuation of the assets and liabilities of the person who has died is completed, at least some of the Inheritance Tax owing must be paid before the Grant of Representation will be issued. In most cases, Inheritance Tax must be paid within six months from the end of the month in which the death occurs, otherwise interest is charged on the amount owing. If you have queries about the calculation of Inheritance Tax and the payment process, you may want to telephone the Inheritance Tax Helpline (on 0845 302 0900). It may be possible to pay Inheritance Tax in instalments or for the executor(s) to obtain a bank loan, repayable eventually from the estate, if immediate payment would otherwise be difficult.

Obtaining details of the assets and debts of the person who has died

As a first step, the personal representatives should list those assets which they know, based on personal observation or what they have found in the papers of the person who has died. The papers will include, for example, bank statements, cheque books, outstanding bills, share certificates and insurance documentation. They should then send notification of the death to financial institutions, such as banks, building societies, insurance companies and the deceased's accountant. The letters to the banks and building societies should request information about each account. Also, personal representatives should ask for a list of deeds and other documents held on behalf of the person who has died; for example, life policies as at the date of death.

Personal representatives do not have to wait to receive the Grant of Representation to begin this notification and inventory, but a copy must be sent to each institution when it is received from the Probate Registry (in England & Wales), the Probate and Matrimonial Office (in Northern Ireland), or the Commissary Department of the Sheriff Court concerned (in Scotland).

The goal is to get in writing the value of all the assets and debts as at the time of death. The information must be provided on the probate or Confirmation forms. Even if an asset is left as a legacy to a beneficiary, it must be listed and accounted for in the inventory.

Valuing assets of the person who has died

Checklist of assets that will often occur

- House or flat
- Bank account
- Stocks and shares
- Businesses
- Car
- Jewellery
- Works of art
- Other possessions
- National savings
- Premium bonds
- Outstanding salary or pension payments
- Life insurance and pension policies
- Taxes and bills
- Social security payments
- Foreign property – there are special arrangements relating to probate if the person who died was living or domiciled abroad. Details may be found at www.direct.gov.uk/en/Rightsandresponsibilities/Death/Preparation/DG_10029716

If you are acting as a personal representative, you should clearly identify where assets are jointly owned and note them on the forms. Generally, the value reported should be the price the asset would fetch if it was sold on the open market on the date of death. You may wish to seek a professional valuation for some of these assets. Before probate is granted, the valuation will be checked by the District Valuer on behalf of HM Revenue & Customs.

Valuing debts of the person who has died

The following is a checklist of debts that the person who has died may owe. Information on any of these liabilities that apply should be included in Section F of Form IHT200.

If necessary, it is generally possible to request a delay in the payment of debts until the Grant has been obtained and funds are available. Personal representatives do not have to pay them out of their own income or savings.

Checklist of debts that will often occur

- Water rates
- Telephone bill
- Electricity bill
- Gas bill
- Loan or overdraft
- Credit card bills
- Mail order catalogue bill
- Rent arrears
- Hire purchase payments
- Debts owed by the person who has died to other individuals
- Outstanding Income Tax and Capital Gains Tax – the principles of taxation which apply are broadly similar across all UK countries. Help Sheet IR 282, *'Deaths, Personal Representatives and Legatees'*, is available from www.hmrc.gov.uk, or from HM Revenue & Customs' offices
- Reasonable funeral expenses

The personal representatives should respond to bills and contact potential creditors by providing formal notification of the death, which will usually require a copy of the death certificate.

Tax

The person administering the estate needs to inform HM Revenue & Customs about the death so that HM Revenue & Customs can assess whether or not the person who has died has paid too much or too little tax. If there is a refund of tax, then HM Revenue & Customs will pay it to the estate of the person who has died. If there is tax due, then it will be a debt on the estate and will need to be paid by the estate.

Most gifts made more than seven years before death are exempt from Inheritance Tax. However, there are specific provisions relating to trusts and companies and it is advisable to check these provisions with HM Revenue & Customs. Further information is available at www.direct.gov.uk/en/Moneytaxandbenefits/taxes/InheritanceTaxEstatesandTrusts/DG_4016736.

Distribution of gifts and legacies from the estate

Once the assets have been identified and all the debts, expenses and taxes have been paid, the personal representative must distribute what is left in the estate to the beneficiaries.

- If there is a valid Will, then the distribution of the residuary estate, after receiving all of the assets and paying the debts, will be according to the wishes of the person who has died, as expressed in the Will.

- If there is no Will or no valid Will, then the distribution of the rest of the estate will be in accordance with the intestacy rules – see below.

Intestacy rules

When the person who dies does not leave a Will, or has a Will that is invalid, he or she has died 'intestate'.

In these circumstances, in England & Wales, distribution of the estate is determined by the Administration of Estates Act 1924, and in Northern Ireland, by the Administration of Estates Act (Northern Ireland) 1955. In Scotland, distribution of the estate is determined by the Succession (Scotland) Act of 1964, as amended.

The rules on inheritance where someone has died intestate are complex and you may wish to seek advice and further information (e.g. from the Citizens' Advice Bureau). Summaries of the intestacy rules applying in the countries of the UK may be found at www.hmrc.gov.uk/manuals/ihtmanual/IHTM12000.htm#4.

If you are using a solicitor or other agent, he or she will be able to deal with this for you.

Possessions of the person who has died

If any of the possessions, such as a car, are subject to a hire purchase or rental agreement, the personal representatives will need to contact the company concerned.

For personal possessions the Will may specify who should receive some or all of the possessions. If there is no Will, then the disposal of the possessions will be subject to the intestacy rules.

You may find that you or others who will receive the possessions may find it difficult to accept them. This may be because the possessions are intricately linked to grieving after bereavement.

Personal and company pensions

- If the person who has died was receiving a pension from an occupational scheme (i.e. a work-related scheme) or a personal pension scheme, then you should contact the administrator of the pension scheme so that the pension can be cancelled. Also, the administrator would determine if there is any under or over payment and if there is any pension payable to any widow or widower or partner or children.

- If the person was not already receiving a pension from an occupational scheme or a personal pension scheme, but had made contributions to such a scheme, then he or she may have a 'deferred pension', which means that the pension has been earned but has not yet been drawn. You will need to contact the administrator of the pension scheme to check the current position.

Financial planning in changed circumstances after the death

After someone dies there may be a drastic change in your income and it may take some time to finalise all your revised income ('incomings') and revised expenditure ('outgoings'). Financial planning and control and budgeting are important in both the short term and long term.

If you have any financial worries (e.g. about paying the mortgage or rent, or paying heating and lighting), it is advisable to contact the creditors (to whom money is owed) as soon as possible. Some creditors may give you the opportunity to reschedule payments. Your local Citizens' Advice Bureau or other relevant agency will be able to assist.

The ability to pay the bills is affected not only by the incomings and outgoings but is also affected by cash flow, i.e. when bills are due to be paid and when income (benefits, pensions, salary, etc.) will be received.

Some people may find it helpful to have an accountant or financial adviser to assist them in financial planning. However, do be careful about the costs of those services and the benefits they may produce.

Looking to the future

In the period immediately following your bereavement, it may be very difficult for you to think beyond the current day, let alone to look forward for weeks or months. Your emotions will probably change over time and also can change from day to day or hour to hour. 'Take each day one day at a time' is sensible advice for most people. Eventually, you will find your own ways of coping.

You may want to think about your memories of the person who has died and ways of commemorating them.

Your landmarks

For most bereaved people, there will be days which are very significant, such as the anniversary of their death, the day which would have been their loved one's birthday, Christmas or other religious festival, family weddings, and so on. These days may always be significant, despite the passage of time, but will usually become less painful and give more opportunities for happy memories too. Everyone has their own way of preparing for these landmarks; sometimes privately, sometimes with family and friends.

It is important to remember that where children were bereaved, their understanding of the situation will change as they get older and it will cause them to seek more information about the death. It is helpful to be as open as possible.

Ways of commemorating the person who has died

There are many kinds of commemoration, in addition to headstones or memorials in a cemetery (see page 32). Some people arrange a memorial ceremony or commemoration, some time after the funeral, so that people who knew or worked with the person who has died are able to celebrate his or her life and achievements. More private commemorations may involve continuing an activity which used to be shared with the person who has died (e.g. going to a football match). Some people like to plant a tree or flowers in their garden or at a more public location.

Donations to charities are sometimes thought of as a kind of memorial, as they enable work to continue which is felt to have relevant significance. If you are thinking of setting up a charity or trust in someone's memory, it is wise to check out the responsibilities this involves and whether there is an existing charity which might take on what you want to achieve.

Other kinds of memorials include community projects set up in the person's name or a gift to the community, such as a bench carrying the person's name, for which a dedication ceremony may be held.

If memories are difficult

As explained in the section of this Kit on the emotional experience of bereavement, there are some circumstances which may give rise to difficult memories. For example, if the death was violent or untimely, if you were a witness to it, or if your relationship with the person who has died was difficult. It is not unusual to experience anger in bereavement (including feeling angry with the person who has died) or to feel a sense of great loss because of a changed future (e.g. the loss of a happy shared retirement).

Consulting your GP, accessing bereavement support or bereavement counselling, or consulting sources of information about bereavement reactions, are examples of strategies which may help you to find out whether you would benefit from further help.

The future

You will never forget the person who has died, but you will find your own balance between living through your grief and building a new life. Many bereaved people, after a period of time, find that they are able to take up new interests and roles, and to make new friends. It is possible to find comfort in your memories and to regain energy, confidence and hope.

Useful contacts

Useful organisations

Brakecare   01484 421 611

Support and advice following a road death.

Cancer Backup   0808 800 1234

Support for anyone affected by the death of someone from cancer.

Childline   0800 11 11

24-hour helpline for children and young people.

Compassionate Friends   0845 123 2304

Website   www.tcf.org.uk

For families in which a child of any age has died.

Cruse Bereavement Care

Day by day helpline   0844 477 9400
Young people's freephone helpline   0808 808 1677
Email   helpline@cruse.org.uk
Young people's website   www.rd4u.org.uk
Main website   www.cruse.org.uk

Cruse Bereavement Care is the national bereavement charity. Cruse Bereavement Care and Cruse Bereavement Care Scotland provide services to anyone who has been bereaved, whatever the circumstances, and whoever has died.

Macmillan Cancer Support   0808 808 2020

Can support families after the death of someone from cancer.

National Association of Widows   0247 663 4848

Roadpeace   0845 450 0355

Website   www.roadpeace.org

Supporting bereaved and injured road crash victims.

Samaritans   0845 790 9090

SANDS (Stillbirth and Neonatal Death Society)   020 7436 5881

Support for parents and other relatives when a baby dies during late pregnancy, at birth, or soon after birth.

SOBS (Survivors of Bereavement by Suicide)   0870 241 3337

Way Foundation   029 207 11209
Website   www.wayfoundation.org.uk

Support for those widowed, under the age of 50 and their children.

Winston's Wish   0845 203 0405
Website   www.winstonswish.org.uk

Support for bereaved children and young people up to the age of 18.

Funeral arrangements and official procedures

Bereavement Register   0870 600 7222
Website   www.the-bereavement-register.org.uk

The Register lists names, addresses and telephone numbers of people who have died and this information is then removed from the databases used by those companies which subscribe to the Bereavement Register.

Coroner
England & Wales   www.dca.gov.uk
Northern Ireland   028 9044 6800
                                         www.coronersni.gov.uk

For details of your local Coroner, contact directory enquiries. The government's Department of Constitutional Affairs has information on the Coroner service. Some local Coroners maintain their own website.

Cremation Society of Great Britain   01622 688 292/3
Website   www.cremation.org.uk

Deaths in Scotland   www.scotland.gov.uk

For the Scottish Executive, which produces the useful booklets, '*What to Do After a Death in Scotland*' and '*What to Do After a Death in Scotland: Social Security Supplement*'.

Foreign and Commonwealth Office   020 7008 1500
Website   www.fco.gov.uk

For assistance after a death overseas.

Government's website	www.direct.gov.uk
Inquest	020 8802 7430

Support and information on problems related to inquests.

Institute of Cemetery and Crematorium Management	020 8989 4661
Website	www.iccm-uk.com
Institute of Civil Funerals	www.iocf.org.uk
National Association of Funeral Directors	0845 230 1343
Website	www.nafd.org.uk
National Association of Memorial Masons	01788 542 264
Email	enquiries@namm.org.uk
Website	www.namm.org.uk
National Society of Allied and Independent Funeral Directors	0845 2306 7777
Website	www.saif.org.uk
Natural Death Centre	0871 288 2098
Website	www.naturaldeath.org.uk

Helps arrange inexpensive, family-organised and environmentally-friendly funerals.

Probate in England & Wales

Court Service website	www.hmcourts-service.gov.uk
Probate Service website	www.hmcourts-service.gov.uk/cms/wills.htm
Probate and Inheritance Tax helpline in England & Wales	0845 302 0900

Probate in Northern Ireland

Belfast and all areas except Londonderry, Tyrone and Fermanagh	028 9072 4678
Londonderry, Tyrone and Fermanagh	028 7126 1832

Probate in Scotland

Contact the nearest Sheriff Court – a list is available at www.scotcourts.gov.uk.

Whether or not there is a Will, contact the local Probate Registry for deaths in England & Wales, the local Sheriff Court for deaths in Scotland and the Probate and Matrimonial Office for deaths in Northern Ireland. Contact details are obtainable from the telephone directory or directory enquiries.

Registrar of Deaths

England & Wales	0151 471 4805
	www.gro.gov.uk
Northern Ireland	www.groni.gov.uk
Scotland	www.gro-scotland.gov.uk

Financial and legal contacts

Capital Taxes Office	020 7603 4622
Website	www.hmrc.gov.uk

Community Legal Service (CLS)	0845 345 4345
Website	www.clsdirect.org.uk

Provides free information, help and advice on a range of common issues.

Enduring Power of Attorney Helpline	0845 330 2963

HM Revenue & Customs' National Insurance Contributions Office	www.hmrc.gov.uk

Has information on National Insurance contributions. See the telephone directory for the telephone number.

Jobcentre Plus	www.jobcentreplus.gov.uk

For the telephone number contact directory enquiries or look at the Jobcentre Plus website. Jobcentre Plus is part of the government's Department for Work and Pensions.

National Bereavement Benefits Helpline	0845 608 8602

Law Centres	020 7387 8570
Website	www.lawcentres.org.uk

They provide a free and independent professional legal service to those who live and work in their catchment areas.

Law Society	
England& Wales	020 7242 1222
Scotland	0131 226 7411
Website	www.lawsociety.org.uk

Occupational Pensions Advisory Service	020 7233 8016

Provides information and guidance on the whole spectrum of pensions covering state, company, personal and stakeholder schemes.

Pension Service (Department for Work and Pensions)	0845 606 0265
Website	www.pensionservice.gov.uk

General contacts

Age Concern	0800 009 966
Website	www.ageconcern.org.uk

Supports all people over the age of 50.

Citizens' Advice Bureau (CAB)	www.citizensadvice.org.uk

You can obtain the telephone number for your local branch of the CAB through directory enquiries or the CAB website. CAB helps people resolve their legal, money and other problems by providing free information and advice.

Environment Agency	0870 850 6506
Email	enquiries@environment-agency.gov.uk
Website	www.environment-agency.gov.uk

Help The Aged	0808 800 6565
Website	www.helptheaged.org.uk

Supports older people.

Human Tissue Authority	020 7211 3400
Website	www.hta.gov.uk

Organ Donation Donor Line	0845 606 0400
Preference Services	0845 703 4599

Most commercial mailing is carried out by companies which belong to the Direct Marketing Association (DMA). The DMA helpline will tell you how to stop unwanted mail, phone calls or faxes.

Shelterline	0808 800 4444
Website	www.shelter.org.uk

Deals with homelessness and all types of housing problems.

Victim Information and Advice Service (Scotland)	0131 226 2626
Website	www.crownoffice.gov.uk/victims

Resources for children and young people

Young people (aged 12–25) can seek support from:

Cruse Bereavement Care Young People's Service
PO Box 800
Richmond TW9 1RG
Helpline: 0808 808 1677 (Freephone)
Email: private@rd4u.org.uk
Website: www.rd4u.org.uk

There is an online and telephone support service for children and young people (aged under 25) who have experienced bereavement. It provides online support through a message board, as well as private email, and the website has an online gallery and timeline for sharing experiences. It also has downloadable information for children and young people.

Children and young people can telephone, write, email or post a message on the board.

The helpline opening hours are: Monday–Friday, 9.30am–5pm.

Free information leaflets, produced by Cruse Bereavement Care, can be found at www.cruse.org.uk/free_leaflets.html. The following may be useful:

- *'After Someone Dies'*

  A leaflet about death, bereavement and grief for young people.

- *'Has Someone Died – Helping Children'*

  A leaflet on how to help grieving children.

A range of publications can be found on the Cruse Bereavement Care website by going to www.cruse.org.uk and then clicking on 'Online Store'. The most popular of these are:

For children:

- *'Badger's Parting Gifts'* by Sue Varley

  Includes coloured illustrations. A wise old badger dies and the other animals miss him, but he lives on in all they learned from him.

- *'Waterbugs and Dragonflies'* by Doris Stickney

  Includes black and white illustrations (which can be coloured by a child). The dragonfly life cycle is told as a story. It has a short, simple ending with a separate section for parents, including a Christian interpretation and a prayer if required.

For parents and carers:

• *'Caring for Bereaved Children'* by Mary Blending

Children feel grief but often show it differently from adults. For parents, relatives, teachers and others, this concise, bestselling Cruse booklet offers insight into a child's grief and suggests ways of helping. It covers age groups from birth up to and including adolescence.

You can obtain further information on books and publications from the Cruse website or by telephoning 020 8939 9530. You can order and pay for them through the online store or by sending an order and payment to Cruse Bereavement Care, PO Box 800, Richmond TW9 1RG.

Template letter to building society

[*Insert your address or letter heading for reply including email address and phone number, if applicable*]

[*Insert bank or building society name and address*]

[*Insert date*]

Dear Sir,

Notification of death of account holder: [*insert full name*]

I am writing to inform you of the sad death of [*insert full name*] of [*insert full address*] on [*insert date of death*]. I am writing as [*insert your role – administrator/executor of the estate*] and [*insert your relationship to the person who has died – widow/widower/ civil partner/son/daughter/brother/sister*].

[*If applicable*] There is a co-executor/administrator who is [*insert name*] of [*insert address*].

Mr/Mrs had [*insert number*] accounts with you [*insert account numbers*].

I enclose the [*insert passbooks/most recent statement*] for these accounts.

Please acknowledge this letter to the address above and inform me of the balances of the accounts at the date of death, including any interest accrued to the date of death.

In order that I can complete the tax affairs, I would be grateful if you would confirm the interest that was credited to the account for the period for the tax year to 5 April before the death.

I enclose [*insert a certified copy of the death certificate for your records*]. [*I enclose the original death certificate; please return this to me at the above address.*]

[*For joint accounts.*] As this was a joint account, please confirm that my access to funds will continue uninterrupted.

[*Where the person who has died was the sole account holder.*] Please inform me as to whether you are prepared to release any funds before the Grant of Administration (probate) [*as these may be required to meet the funeral expenses*]. [*As all household bills were normally paid from this account, I would appreciate your assistance in ensuring that I am able to access the funds to meet my immediate living expenses.*]

If you have any queries, please do not hesitate to contact me on [*insert telephone number*].

Thank you for your assistance, which is much appreciated at this difficult time.

Yours sincerely,

[*Insert your name*]
[*Executor/administrator*]

Template letter to pension scheme

[*Insert your address or letter heading for reply including email address and phone number, if applicable*]

[*Insert pension provider's name and address*]

[*Insert date*]

Dear Sir,

Notification of death of pension scheme member: [*insert full name*]

I am writing to inform you of the sad death of [*insert full name*] of [*insert full address*] on [*insert date of death*]. I am writing as [*insert your role – administrator/executor of the estate*] and [*insert your relationship to the person who has died – widow/widower/ civil partner/son/daughter/brother/sister*].

I understand that payment of the pension due to [*insert name*] will cease at the date of death. Please ensure that payment is made to this date and, if applicable, inform me of any overpayment and action to be taken.

[*I understand that as the [widow/widower/civil partner] I may be entitled to payments from the pension scheme, and would be grateful for your assistance in informing me as to how to make my claim*] [*for any lump sum or pension payable.*]

Please can you also provide me with details of the gross pension and tax paid in this tax year.

I enclose [*insert a certified copy of the death certificate for your records*]. [*I enclose the original death certificate; please return this to me at the above address.*]

If you have any queries, please do not hesitate to contact me on [*insert telephone number*].

Yours sincerely,

[*Insert your name*]
[*Executor/administrator*]

Notes

Notes

FUNERALS – SOME IDEAS AND ISSUES

Further information is contained in the Manual section on funerals

All the choices you make about a funeral will be affected by what you know about the wishes of the person who has died, by your own wishes, and those of close family and friends.

THE CEREMONY

- An early issue to consider is whether to employ a funeral director; if you are doing so, it is wise to check that the firm you have selected is a member of a professional association with a code of practice.

- If you are employing a funeral director and do not feel up to the task of visiting their premises, ask for a home visit.

- Before employing a funeral director be sure that you know which services they are providing and what the costs will be. Request a written quotation. You may want to consider obtaining a quotation from more than one funeral director. If you then decide to engage a funeral director, you are entering into a contract; take all the time you need to consider this.

- Is the person who has died going to be cremated or buried?

  _____

- If you arrange a cremation, do you know what is to happen to your loved one's ashes or are you asking the funeral director to retain the ashes until you have decided?

  _____

  _____

- How is your loved one to be dressed? Their own clothes, or clothes provided by the funeral home? Would you like to keep a lock of the hair of the person who has died?

  _____

  _____

- What type of ceremony to have? Religious or non-religious? Or a mixture of content?

  _____

  _____

- Where will the ceremony be? Or will there be a burial or cremation ceremony and an earlier ceremony as well?

  _____

  _____

- Who will lead the ceremony or ceremonies?

  _____

  _____

- Who else will contribute to the ceremony? Do you want someone to contribute a tribute to the person who has died?

  _____

  _____

- Would you want any family members or friends to carry the coffin?

  _____

- Should children attend the funeral?

  _____

- Do you want music at the ceremony and if so, what music?

  _____

- Would you like flowers or charitable donations, or a mixture of both?

  _____

- Would you like a printed order of service for the ceremony?

  _____

- What transport arrangements are you making for the close family, extended family, friends and colleagues? Do you want the cortege to leave from a family residence or from the residence of the person who has died?

  _____

  _____

MEETING FUNERAL COSTS

- How much you want to spend will depend on the type of ceremony you want and how much you can afford.
- Possible sources of funds may be a funeral pre-payment plan, the estate of the person who has died, or the pension scheme of the person who has died. Family and friends may be prepared to contribute to the costs.
- You may be eligible for a bereavement payment from the Government (this is only payable to those under retirement age).
- A payment from the Social Fund will be a loan.

AFTER THE FUNERAL ...

- You may want to have an opportunity after the funeral ceremony to be with family and friends, or you may prefer to be alone. Some people invite a wide circle of friends; others prefer just to be with a close circle.
- The type of gathering could range from a buffet meal at someone's home to, for example, a larger occasion at a hotel or restaurant.
- When thinking about whether to have a gathering and if so, what type of gathering try to weigh up what you want, what others may want and what you can afford.

IF ANYTHING GOES WRONG

- Most funerals go smoothly and are a source of comfort. Should you have grounds for complaint, however, the professional associations in the funeral industry have complaints procedures, or you may wish to seek help from Citizens' Advice or from the Trading Standards Department of your local authority.

BEREAVEMENT IS A MOST DIFFICULT TIME, WHETHER YOU HAVE BEEN DIRECTLY AFFECTED YOURSELF, OR WHETHER YOU ARE TRYING TO HELP ANOTHER BEREAVED PERSON.

WHAT HELPS

Cruse Bereavement Care is contacted by a bereaved person, or by someone concerned about a bereaved person, every three minutes. Here are some of the things that people have told us they have found helpful – you may have other ideas which will be based on what you know about yourself or about someone you are trying to help.

'I appreciated the letters people wrote'
Try to write a letter to someone who is bereaved; if you have received condolence letters, keep those you have found most helpful, as you may want to reread them.

'I wanted to talk over and over again'
If you are bereaved, then try talking to trusted friends or family members; this may help to help relieve some of the stress. If you know of someone who has been bereaved, try to be there as a patient listener for that person.

'I wanted people to say they knew what had happened'
If you are with a bereaved person, try not to avoid the bereavement or pretend you do not know or do not want to talk about the bereavement. The person will appreciate your care. If you feel that you do not know what to say to them, a simple expression of concern will be enough.

'I needed someone to tell me what to do'
If you are bereaved, then try not to be afraid to ask for help about practical and financial matters and if you are helping a bereaved person, try to offer to help with the practical and financial matters, or to suggest other sources of help.

'I wanted time off work'
Try to be honest with your employer if you have been bereaved and ask them to help in any way they are able.

'Sometimes I needed to be busy, but other times it was great when people offered to help'

'I kept some special things that remind me of the good times we spent together'

'I realised that this was the one time I couldn't cope on my own and I learned to accept help'

Be careful about driving or operating machinery; under the stress of bereavement, these tasks may become more difficult.

These simple actions will not remove the pain of bereavement, but they may help you to get through each day and each week, particularly at first. Do not be surprised if progress is slow; bereavement reactions are powerful, and may include:

FEAR – for example, fear of being left alone; fear of 'breaking down' or 'losing control'; and fear of another death occurring.

HELPLESSNESS – for example, feeling helpless because you could not prevent the death; feeling helpless because you do not have enough energy to do the practical things; and feeling helpless because you are relying on others to do things for you.

SADNESS – for example, for the dead person because their death was untimely; because they were in pain; because the death was sudden; and because you have been left behind to cope.

LONGING – for example, longing to see the person again; and longing to be at peace with them.

GUILT – for example, regrets for things not done; guilt at not being able to cope; and guilt at not crying.

SHAME – for example, shame for having been exposed as helpless, emotional and needing others; and shame for having not reacted as you would have wished.

ANGER – for example, anger at what has happened; anger at how it happened; anger at anyone who might be to blame for the death; and anger expressed as 'why has this happened to me?'

MEMORIES – a death may prompt feelings about a previous death or loss.

LET DOWN – for example, disappointment for all the plans that cannot be fulfilled; it may take some time for you to begin to have any hope for the future.

NUMBNESS – some people who have been bereaved talk about a numbness, which may sometimes be their bodies trying to protect themselves from the pain of the loss of the person who has died.

FLASHBACKS – if you were present when the person died or soon afterwards, you may have flashbacks with very strong images of what you saw.

DREAMS – some people will dream about the person and then wake up and suddenly realise that they have died.

PHYSICAL SYMPTOMS – after a profound shock you may find that you experience symptoms such as loss of appetite, difficulty in sleeping or exhaustion. At some time you may want to talk to your doctor.

ACCIDENTS – a death may become the main thing that you think about for some time and the stress of this and the difficulty in focusing on other things may make you more accident-prone.

ALCOHOL AND DRUGS – the extra tension after the death of someone may lead you to increase your intake of substances which you might feel dull the pain of the bereavement. If this is happening to an extent that worries you, it may be wise to seek help.

CRUSE BEREAVEMENT CARE

Cruse can provide:

- Someone to talk to – the opportunity to talk once or more with a trained Bereavement Volunteer.

- Groups which offer bereaved people the chance to talk with others in similar circumstances.

- Information on many aspects of bereavement, including practical and financial matters.

- Advice about children and young people. Cruse can support parents and others who want to know how best to respond to children and teenagers who have been affected by death.

- Information about other bereavement organisations.

- Training, support, information and publications for anyone interested in the best way to help others as well as themselves, including bereaved children.

Cruse has two national helplines:

- Cruse Helpline – 0844 477 9400
- Freephone Helpline for Young People – 0808 808 1677

and two websites:

- **www.cruse.org.uk** where there is information about Cruse's services including local services across England, Wales and Northern Ireland. Also on the website there are downloadable leaflets and printed publications for sale.

- **www.rd4u.org.uk** which is for young people and has many useful resources including a message board facility.

WHEN TO SEEK FURTHER HELP

As we have explained above, strong reactions to bereavement are normal. You may wish, however, to speak to your doctor or take other advice if you feel that your emotions are not falling into place over a period of time, or if you continue to feel chronic tension, confusion, emptiness or exhaustion. Other reasons for seeking help might include you suffering flashbacks, persistent sleeplessness, or various physical symptoms. Your GP or NHS Direct are good places to start.

WHAT TO DO FOLLOWING A DEATH – CHECKLIST

Government Leaflet D49, *What to Do After a Death in England and Wales*, gives detailed information and help when someone has died. This checklist provides a summary of some important things you need to deal with. Often, there is a lot to think about and you cannot be expected to do everything straightaway. The tick boxes provided should help you, or the person helping you, to keep a note of what you have already done.

Before referring to this list, it is very useful to have the following information about the person who has died. This will make the task of completing any forms or documents much easier.

- Date of birth/place of birth ☐
- Date of marriage or civil partnership (if appropriate) ☐
- National Insurance number ☐
- NHS number ☐
- Child Benefit number ☐
- Tax reference number ☐

IN THE FIRST FIVE DAYS

You cannot be expected to inform everyone of the person's death straightaway. However, it is important to do the following in the first five days:

- Notify the family doctor ☐
- Register the death at the Register Office ☐
- Contact a funeral director to begin funeral arrangements ☐
  if the person who has died was receiving any
  benefits or tax credits, you must advise the office that
  was paying the benefit.
- Complete Form BD8, which the Registrar supplies ☐
  and send it to the local Jobcentre Plus, Social
  Security or pensions office. You can find
  the address in your phone book

A death needs to be registered within five days. However, in some circumstances the Registrar will extend this time limit, usually when the Coroner is involved. The death may be registered anywhere in the country, but it is generally registered in the area where the death occurred. Please note that the Registrar will also ask for the details of the deceased's mother, but if these are not known it will not prevent registration. Some organisations will want to see an original death certificate. The Registrar can supply more than one certificate, but there is a charge for this service.

BENEFITS AND TAX CREDITS

If you, or the person who has died, were receiving any benefits or tax credits, it is important to tell the office paying the benefit as soon as possible. You can find a telephone number and address in your phone book. The paying office will have to reassess your benefit entitlement, as your circumstances have now changed. By doing this, you can prevent overpayments of benefit and also check any other benefits that you may be entitled to, such as bereavement benefits or the Social Fund Funeral Payment. You can find out more about these benefits below.

List of people it is best to tell as soon as possible:

- Bank/building society/post office ☐
- Employer ☐
- Friends ☐
- Hire purchase or loan companies ☐
- Credit card providers/store cards ☐
- Jobcentre Plus or local Social Security Office ☐
- Landlord ☐
- Local authority ☐
- Pension providers/insurance companies ☐
- HM Revenue & Customs ☐
- School ☐
- Solicitor ☐
- Social Services ☐

DEALING WITH THE ESTATE

- If the deceased named you as executor in his or her Will, you may need to obtain a Grant of Probate to administer the deceased's estate.
- If the deceased did not leave a Will and there is a need for you to handle the deceased's estate, then you should find out whether you are eligible to apply for a Grant of Letters of Administration to administer the deceased's estate.

For information, contact the Probate and Inheritance Tax helpline on 0845 30 20 900.

Other things you may have to do:

- Cancel direct debits
- Cancel any credit or store cards
- Cancel insurance policies

THINGS TO SEND BACK OR CANCEL

When returning any documents, enclose a note of explanation giving details about the person who has died and the date of death.

- Any payable orders or cheques to Jobcentre Plus or the Social Security office or tax credit office. This applies to all benefits, including Child Benefit ☐
- Passport – return to the deceased's regional Passport Office. Check for details at www.ukpa.gov.uk or phone the Passport Adviceline on 0870 521 0410 ☐
- Driving licence – return to DVLA, Longview Road, Swansea SA6 7JL ☐
- Car registration documents – return to DVLA (as above). Change of ownership may have to be recorded ☐
- Season ticket(s) – claim any refund(s) due ☐
- Library – return any books ☐
- Club membership – claim any refund(s) due ☐
- Trade union – claim any refund due ☐
- Subscriptions to magazines or newspapers ☐
- Home Help service or Meals on Wheels ☐
- Dentist ☐

- Domestic utility providers: gas, water and electricity ☐
- Car insurance ☐
- Disabled parking permit – contact the deceased's local authority ☐
- The Bereavement Register – removes names and addresses of people ☐
  who have died.

BENEFITS

BEREAVEMENT BENEFITS

If you are widowed or become a surviving civil partner, you may be entitled to bereavement benefits. You may claim these benefits even if you are working.

All bereavement benefit claims must be made on Form BB1. You can get this form from your local Jobcentre Plus office or from the website at www.jobcentreplus.gov.uk.

It is important to note that there are time limits affecting all benefit claims. If you apply too late, it may affect the amount you receive or you may receive nothing at all.

BEREAVEMENT BENEFITS TIME LIMITS

Bereavement Allowance/Widowed Parent's Allowance* must be claimed within three months of the death of your spouse or civil partner.

*Please note: In order to receive Widowed Parent's Allowance you must be the main Child Benefit payee. If your late spouse or civil partner was the main payee for Child Benefit, you will need to reclaim Child Benefit in your own name. Please do so without delay. Child Benefit contact details are noted below.

Bereavement Payment must be claimed within 12 months of the death of your spouse or civil partner.

CHILD BENEFIT

Child Benefit is a benefit paid to people who are bringing up children.

CHILD BENEFIT TIME LIMITS

If a child has died, HM Revenue and Customs must be told within eight weeks. Payment of Child Benefit for the child who has died will continue to be paid for eight weeks after death.

You can tell HM Revenue & Customs:

In writing:

Child Benefit Office
PO Box 1
Newcastle upon Tyne
NE88 1AA

Email: Child.Benefit@hmrc.gsi.gov.uk
Telephone: 0845 302 1444
Textphone: 0845 302 1474
Website: www.hmrc.gov.uk/childbenefit

SOCIAL FUND

You may be able to get a Social Fund Funeral Payment to help you with the cost of the funeral.

You can claim this payment on Form SF200, which you can get from a Jobcentre Plus office or from the website at www.jobcentreplus.gov.uk.

SOCIAL FUND TIME LIMITS

The time limit for claiming this payment is three months.

BENEFITS CHECKLIST

It is important to remember that all benefits have time limits and if you apply too late it may affect the amount you receive or you may receive nothing at all. The checklist below can be used to make a note of any benefits you may want to claim.

- Do you want to claim any benefits? ☐ Yes ☐ No

If you ticked yes, which of the following benefits do you want to claim?

- Bereavement benefits ☐
- Social Fund Funeral Payment ☐
- Child Benefit ☐
- Guardian's Allowance ☐
- Income Support ☐
- Jobseeker's Allowance ☐
- Pension Credit ☐
- Industrial Injuries Disablement Benefit ☐
- Tax Credits ☐
- Housing Benefit ☐
- Council Tax Benefit ☐

P2250709520